Got t
POW

Got the POWER

7 Tools to Produce the Work Life You Want

CIE MURRAY

LIFESOURCE PUBLISHING
Atlanta, Georgia

DEDICATION

I dedicate this book to
S. Charles Murray, my husband,
covenant partner, and the love of my life.
Thank you for your unwavering,
unconditional love and support.
I thank God for bringing you into my life.

CONTENTS

Acknowledgments

I would like to express my gratitude to the individuals who supported me in bringing this book to fruition.

To Mae M. Gilley, my human resources consultant, for your inspiration and reassurance.

To Brookes Nohlgren, copyeditor and production proofer, for your candor and amazingly sharp eyes.

To Dotti Albertine, book designer, for making the cover pop.

To Reta Trent, for your enthusiasm and constant encouragement.

To the many individuals who contributed in your own special way: Adjo Amekudzi, Sybil Freeman, Darcel Ivey, Alexis Jackson, Kathryn Keesee, Eric McMath, and Annamarie Popescu.

You've Got the Power!

*Y*ou MAY THINK you don't have the power to obtain the work life you want, but you have more power than you think. Unfortunately, many people lose hope for a fulfilling work life and thus spend one-third of their lives unengaged and unfulfilled. When this happens, it's not just workers who suffer—so do their organizations. Deprived of motivated employees, some companies aren't able to be productive or efficient enough to remain competitive in the global economy.

Whether you are an entry-level associate, a vice president reporting to the CEO, or a job seeker, you can have a fulfilling, engaging, and productive work life. But it all begins with you. In this book, I share a seven-tool process that will revolutionize your work life. It will become a work life where you'll thank God it's Monday not thank God it's Friday. A work life in which you will experience the fulfillment that comes with success and accomplishment. A work life where you can cultivate delight and affection for your work.

How does this seven-tool process work? With the first two tools, you'll discover hidden value as you explore what makes you the special person you were born to be. Then you'll complete a survey to determine your Thinker Locator™ Profile. Your profile will give you a good understanding of what motivates, drives, and inspires you to do the things you do. With your Thinker Locator Profile, you will be able to better match your talents and abilities with work tasks, assignments, and jobs that are right for you.

Tools Three, Four, and Five are the workplace action tools. You will be given techniques to use in your daily work life that will help you make better decisions and choices as an employee or leader to enhance your relationships with co-workers, clients, team members, and staff. In addition, you'll find tips and ideas designed to produce creativity, productivity, effectiveness, and success. Tool Six is the fuel you'll need to stay persistent in obtaining the work you want. The last tool provides a mechanism for managing challenges, boosting morale, and overcoming obstacles in your workplace.

When your work life is empowered, so is the rest of your life. You've got the power, you just need to turn it on.

CHAPTER 1

Empowerment Tool of the Believer
Accept the Person You Were Born to Be

"To be nobody-but-yourself in a world which is doing
its best, night and day, to make you everybody else—
means to fight the hardest battle which any
human being can fight; and never stop fighting."

—E. E. CUMMINGS

RICHARD, MY NEPHEW, was working at one of the Top Ten Fortune 500 companies in America. His boss and co-workers liked him and his work. But outside of the company, Richard would talk about how he really wanted to move to Orlando so he could work on his golf game year-round. His goal was to make golf his profession. Some friends and family members discouraged him, feeling this choice was too risky. Eventually, though, he overrode their comments and made the move. A few weeks after Richard arrived in Orlando, while on the course playing golf, a man approached him about his game. The man said, "I really like your swing," then asked, "have you ever thought about doing television commercials?" "No," Richard answered. It

The Empowerment Tool of the Believer is having enough confidence to be your best self, to be the person you were born to be.

turned out that this man was a producer of commercials for Nike. He offered Richard a contract to be the body-double for Tiger Woods. This opened up a sea of golf opportunities for Richard. All because he dared to believe in his best self.

The Empowerment Tool of the Believer is having enough confidence to be your best self, to be the person you were born to be. Let's face it, we live in a society that encourages us to emulate others. We get pressure from the media to dress and drive like movie stars, even if we can't afford it. Our parents have influenced us too. Some of us were told that we could be anything we wanted to be as long as we were willing to work hard, get good grades, and go to college. Then we have our friends who want us to do what they're doing—even when, deep down, we don't want to.

Success and fulfillment come from being *your* best self, not the best somebody else. There is only one you. Each of us was designed with a uniqueness no one else has. No one else has the same eyes, same fingerprints or foot-prints, same hair, same thinking, same gifts and talents. Yet we live in a world that shuns and discourages those who stand up to be themselves.

How have we allowed ourselves to be molded into being someone other than who we really are? For some it may have started at home, when parents encouraged us to be like a sibling or the girl next door. For others, it began at school with an education system that indicated that we weren't smart because we didn't excel academically. Some of us were influenced by a society that places more value on a career of notoriety, such as a movie star or an athlete, than on a career in teaching or that requires scientific talents.

Many times we miss being our best self when we focus on what someone else is doing. I did this often while working in radio sales. My manager would send a report showing the sales performance of each member of our team. When I read the reports, I would immediately com-pare my performance with that of my

Success and fulfillment come from being your best self, not the best somebody else.

*If you attempt to be better than your associates, you'll only be second best to them. **Why?** Because they are already who they are, their best selves.*

colleagues. Now, there is nothing wrong with using others' performance benchmarks to pull your performance up to a higher level. The problem comes when you attempt to be better than someone else rather than be the best you. When I tried to outperform the star salesperson at the radio station, I didn't realize I was manufacturing unnecessary anxiety and internal pressure. Then, one day in a meeting I heard someone say, "The only sound comparison is between me as I am and me as I used to be." When I started to make comparisons between my current and previous performance levels, I was resetting my goals based on *my* reality and not somebody else's. When I set goals to outperform my past performance, I eventually got closer to becoming the best possible me. Building on being my best self was the only way to do this.

When you compare yourself to others, you won't be able to put your energy into being your best self. If you attempt to be better than your associates, you'll only be second best to them. Why?

Because they are already who they are, their best selves.

CELEBRATE WHO YOU ARE

While I don't know exactly who you are, I do know that you are not what you do for a living. You are not what you have— your car, your house, your pets. Nor are you what other people think about you. Who you are does not come from anything or anyone outside of yourself; it comes from inside you. If you are walking around believing that you are a salesman who works for XYZ Corporation, a husband living in a 3-bedroom house with a wife, two kids, and a dog, driving a Buick, you're missing it. Who are you if all of these externals no longer existed? What are the natural gifts, talents, abilities that make up you? What's your personality like? What are your interests? What truly motivates you from within? What makes you tick? What do you believe in? What do you value? What makes you the special person you are? You may be different from others, but what you bring to the table

You may be different from others, but what you bring to the table is just as valuable as what anybody else brings.

is just as valuable as what anybody else brings.

...you may fall down, but each time you get back up, the stronger your confidence will grow in accepting the person you were born to be.

THE HINDRANCES YOU'LL NEED TO OVERCOME

There are three intrinsic elements you will need to face and overcome in order to build confidence in being your best self. The first one is fear. What fears are you allowing to stop you? Are you afraid of stepping out of your comfort zone? Even though I knew I was designed to use my speaking abilities to encourage groups of people, I resisted it. I had gotten very comfortable being behind the scenes. Although I was dissatisfied with my work life at that point, the uncertainty of the unknown was keeping me in it. To get into my power zone, I had to face my fear of moving out of my comfort zone.

I've heard it said, "Fear comes from focusing on the negative things that could happen." What are you focusing on? Are you fearful of the *what ifs*? "What if I fail?" "What if I make a mistake?" "What if speaking up gets held against me?" "What if I'm not accepted by others?" "What if management doesn't like the way I handle that assignment?" Or you may have the "What if I succeed?" fear. Instead of focusing on the negative that might happen, focus on the good that could occur. Concentrate on accomplishing your goals rather than on the fear.

Moving from fear to being your best self doesn't happen by standing still. It comes about by taking one step at a time. Sometimes these may even be baby steps. In fact, attempting your first few steps may feel like being a wobbly toddler. This is normal. Just keep stepping. As you continue to move forward, you will uncover talents and gifts that have been lying dormant in your heart. These talents may be just the impetus needed to propel your employees, clients, employer, even associates to the next level. Furthermore, you will discover a joy unlike any you've felt before. Sure, once in a while you may fall down, but each time you get back up, the stronger your confidence will grow in accepting the person you were born to be.

Stepping out to be your best self may feel like a risk you can't afford to take. But I would argue the contrary: that it's a risk you can't afford *not* to take. Alfreda Bradley-Coar took a risk when she was assigned the task of introducing Jeffrey Immelt, chairman of General Electric, to an audience of 1,500 people. Instead of following the script she was given, she decided to do an impromptu introduction. Using the techniques standard for evaluating all GE employees, she

"I can"

thoughts are

even more

powerful…

Why? *Because*

"I can" propels

you to take

the kind of

action that

will generate

successful

outcomes…

gave Immelt a performance evaluation based on his own concept of risk-taking. Her speech wooed the audience, especially Immelt. Now guess who's on Immelt's radar screen? That's right, Alfreda Bradley-Coar. All because she dared to be her best self.

Another intrinsic element that may be robbing you of being your best self is the "I can't" belief. This inner self-defeating programming will remind you of what someone said you can't do, can't be, or can't have. "You can't get that promotion; you've never supervised anyone." "You can't take on that project; you don't have enough experience." The real damage occurs when you begin to agree with those thoughts by making your own excuses. "I'm too old to do that." "I'm too young." "I can't; the economy is bad." "I've just not been able to embrace the technology age." "I don't have enough money to go back to school." "That's fine for Sandy to do, but I can't. I'm just not smart enough." It's possible that you've been using "I can't" for so long that you are now applying it to being your best self.

Bobby Scales experienced "I can't" thoughts too. After playing in the minor league for 11 years, at the age of 31, he finally got an offer to play Major League Baseball for the Chicago Cubs. In an interview on ESPN Chicago, Scales said, "I'm not going to sit here and lie to you. There's no question, you have doubts. You do different things, you play different places, and you're like, 'Man, am I ever gonna make it? Is somebody gonna give me a shot?' Yeah, you doubt it, but at the end of the day, it goes back to, do you really believe? If you really believe, then you put those doubts in the back of your mind and you just keep grinding."

Most times when we undergo change, there is pain...

"I can't" thoughts are powerful. Powerful enough to keep you in the past, holding you back from experiencing the work life you want. But do you know that "I can" thoughts are even more powerful? Why? Because "I can" propels you to take the kind of action that will generate successful outcomes now and in the future, which will take you to higher levels in your work life.

The third intrinsic element that can halt your best self is emotional pain.

A few months ago, after I had finished giving a speech, a woman in the audience approached me and asked my opinion on a career decision she was vacillating about. The management in her organization recognized her leadership abilities and wanted to promote her. She realized that this was a great opportunity, but was torn about whether she truly wanted the new responsibilities her promotion would entail. Actually, she had recently been contemplating doing something totally unrelated to her current profession. After talking with her for a little while, I detected that she was experiencing the emotional pain of unpleasant feelings, and internal confusion over the prospective change. Are you allowing the emotional pain of change to stop you from being your authentic self?

Most times when we undergo change, there is pain. This is true even when the change is good for us or is what we have wanted. As the saying goes, "No pain, no gain." When you begin to let go of parts of your old self to make room for becoming your best self, you will experience emotional pain. I remember the first time I went jogging. I thought my legs were going to buckle underneath my body. The next morning the pain was even worse, and every time I moved my legs I felt like crying. Had I allowed that pain to stop me from trying it again, I would have never experienced the exhilaration that comes from jogging consistently over a period of time. How did I do it? I faced the pain by *feeling* it.

You can face the emotional pain of change by allowing yourself to *feel* it. Feelings of sadness and loss will not kill you. It may feel like the emotional pain will kill you, but it won't. However, if you don't face the pain, it will kill your desire and ambition and you will not find a work life you love. Feel the pain, and you'll be able to face the change and get the reward. Go ahead and embrace the pain of unfamiliar territory—new roles, new tasks, new people, the authentic you. Allow the pain to move you forward to being your best you.

THE JOY OF BEING YOUR BEST SELF

There are lots of in-joy moments with being your best self. There's joy from going after the tasks and jobs you really want rather than settling for tasks or jobs that don't fit. You'll experience the joy of liking the person you were created to be. Your creative juices will flow better. Joy also comes from being freed from the control of others' expectations of who they think you should be. You'll be more at peace with your work, making a mark on the world in a manner that no one else could possibly do.

EMPOWERMENT THOUGHTS

- Another person's best self is not better than my best self. They have their purpose and I have mine. I will strive to be my best self, not compete with somebody else's best.

- When I start to think, "I can't," I strike out the "t" and say, "I can."

- I will not make any more excuses. I am taking the initiative, even if it means mere baby steps, toward being my best self.

- I concentrate on the joy I will experience when I operate in being my best self.

To receive your free in-depth
Empowerment Thought,
log on to www.ciemurray.com.

CHAPTER 2

Empowerment Tool of the Thinker
Uncover Your Best Self

"Every good thought you think is contributing
its share to the ultimate result of your life."
—GRENVILLE KLEISER

AFTER WORKING IN RADIO SALES for a couple of years, I began to get bored and desired more excitement in my life. I needed a change. One day the thought came to me, "Cie, why don't you leave Atlanta and move to Houston?" Feeling adventurous, I acted on that thought by taking a week of my vacation to seek similar employment in Houston.

On Monday, the first day of my job search, I had four interviews. The next day I had three more, plus a broadcast association networking event. My prospects for a new job in Houston looked extremely promising. But on Wednesday morning when I woke up, I felt just like I was in Atlanta. I was agitated and grumpy, just plain ole yucky. It suddenly occurred to me that moving was not going to make me happy. Why? I would be taking the same Thinker with me to Houston.

The Thinker represents the thoughts of the head and the thoughts of the heart. The Empowerment Tool of the Thinker is rethinking your thoughts to be your best self. It entails replacing old limiting thoughts with new limitless thoughts. Gratefully, I realized I had to overhaul my Thinker before making my move to Houston. So, I cancelled my remaining interviews and went to the beach. Rethinking your way to becoming your best self begins with rethinking your thoughts about yourself. What are you thinking about yourself right now?

A very wise man once commented, "Would you change a baby's diaper by putting a new diaper on top of the soiled one?" Of course not. You would replace the old diaper with a new diaper. That's because everybody knows that the stink would eventually just seep out from under the diaper. Yet that's exactly what I was about to do. I was about to put new conditions and circumstances on top of

The Empowerment Tool of the Thinker is rethinking your thoughts to be your best self.

my Stinker Thinker. I didn't need a new job or to relocate. I needed to rethink my Thinker.

Until your Thinker (the thoughts of your head and heart) changes, your work life will not change, at least not for long. Your company might give you a raise, an office with a big window, or allow you to work from home. But within a few months or perhaps even days, your unhappy quotient about your work and life will return.

DISCOVER YOUR THINKER LOCATOR PROFILE

Every one of us was born with innate motivational thinking work traits(s). This refers to the manner of thinking that drives our behavior. The Thinker Locator Profile identifies the way we naturally work and tackle problems. An awareness of your Thinker Locator Profile is the first step to becoming your best self.

I developed the Thinker Locator Profile to help you identify the innate

It's not our gender, the generation in which we were born, or even our race or ethnic background that makes us unique.

motivating forces that shape your thinking and behavior toward work. It's not our gender, the generation in which we were born, or even our race or ethnic background that makes us unique. We are unique because of the way we think! Yet, at the same time, it is the manner in which we think that makes us very much the same. So, someone of Asian descent in Beijing, China, for example, may be very similar to someone of European descent in Cheyenne, Wyoming, because they have similar patterns of thinking. The Thinker Locator Profile will help you understand this aspect of you.

WHY A THINKER LOCATOR PROFILE FOR YOU?

As noted, uncovering your Thinker Locator Profile will help you better understand what inspires you to do what you do and your motivation for approaching your work the way you do. It will enable you to direct your abilities toward work that draws upon your passions, which ultimately will bring the greatest benefits to both you and your employer. Understanding your profile will also help you better select work tasks, roles, and careers that match your talents and abilities. And it's when using your Thinker Locator Profile in doing your work that you will experience your greatest sense of accomplishment and satisfaction.

For leaders, an understanding of the Thinker Locator Profile can also help place others in work roles and assignments that allow them to be their best selves. Workers who are given tasks that utilize their innate interests and talents do their best work and produce the best results. The Thinker Locator Profile recognizes the diversity of thinking styles by honoring the individual's ideas and unique methods of working, thus creating work environments where each worker knows that their contribution is valuable to the success of the company. They gain respect for their contribution no matter their work role. As a result, when workers are aware of and act out of their primary Thinker Locator Profile, organizations are better able to achieve their mission and goals.

To clarify, the Thinker Locator Profile is not about competency skills, but rather how people naturally function at work and in life. And no one particular profile is better than another. The best way I've found to think of it is like the different parts of the human body. Feet and hands certainly have different functions, but each serves an important function. If the hands suddenly looked down at the feet and complained, "I'm

Workers who are given tasks that utilize their innate interests and talents do their best work and produce the best results.

When you step over into another Thinker Locator Profile that is not truly you, you don't function as well and you tend to not be as fulfilled and satisfied in your work.

tired of doing all the work, washing this body, the car, cooking, mopping floors, answering correspondence. You've got it easy, just carrying the legs around. I want your job. Let's switch," it wouldn't take long for the body to malfunction. Fingers would find they are not strong enough to handle the weight of the entire body and toes are not agile for returning text messages. Each are suited for their particular tasks.

Doesn't that happen sometimes in our workplaces? A person who has a primary Thinker Locator Profile as "Hands" decides to take on the position of "Feet." Most times when this happens the Hands doesn't realize she's getting ready to move out of her area of strength into one of weakness. We all have been equipped with different gifts, just as the different parts of the body have. When you step over into another Thinker Locator Profile that is not truly you, you don't function as well and you tend to not be as fulfilled and satisfied in your work.

To identify your Thinker Locator Profile, please take the time to complete the questionnaires on the following pages. You'll be glad you did, for you'll gain a better understanding of what drives you to do what you do, how and why you do things differently from your co-workers and associates, and you'll achieve a greater acceptance of who you are. When each worker utilizes their Thinker Locator Profile, both the employee and the workplace function better. Hands are doing what they do best, while feet are being the best feet they can be.

INSTRUCTIONS FOR COMPLETING THE THINKER LOCATOR PROFILE QUESTIONNAIRE

The Thinker Locator Profile is made up of seven motivational thinking work traits: 1) Hands, 2) Brain, 3) Mouth, 4) Arms, 5) Feet, 6) Heart, and 7) Ears-Eyes. These represent the innate traits that constantly drive how we function as we engage at work and life.

As you are completing the surveys, shift your focus from the work you are currently doing to your childhood between the ages of five and eight or younger. What did you like doing? Who did you like spending time with? What did you get in trouble for? For example, Henry Ford got in trouble for taking his birthday watch apart. (Fortunately, he was able to put it back together!)

If you can't remember that far back, speak with the

adults who were involved in your childhood. Pull out pictures, family photo albums, and videos. Reflect on the activities you were involved in.

Why go back that far? Because those were the times when you were probably allowed to be yourself, before adults (though mostly well-meaning) began to influence you to be someone else.

On the surveys, draw a circle around the number for each characteristic that best applies to you. Add up each circled number and write the amount in the Total Profile Score blank. Turn to the Thinker Locator Profile Score Chart on page 40 and write in your Top 3 Total Profile Scores. These are your three primary Thinker Locator Profiles.

THINKER LOCATOR™ PROFILE QUESTIONNAIRES

THINKER LOCATOR™ PROFILE					
Draw a circle around the number for each characteristic that best applies to you					
HANDS PROFILE	*all the time*	*most of the time*	*usually*	*some of the time*	*rarely*	*never*
---	---	---	---	---	---	---
1. Is drawn naturally to hospitality.	5	4	3	2	1	0
2. Likes to finish projects quickly.	5	4	3	2	1	0
3. Finds it hard to turn down requests.	5	4	3	2	1	0
4. Dislikes disorganization and clutter.	5	4	3	2	1	0
5. Is detail oriented; remembers small details.	5	4	3	2	1	0
6. Loves pitching in to help others.	5	4	3	2	1	0
7. Prefers doing projects that require use of hands.	5	4	3	2	1	0
8. Loves assisting those you support to be successful.	5	4	3	2	1	0
9. Rather work on short-term, immediate projects.	5	4	3	2	1	0
10. Has a strong need to be appreciated.	5	4	3	2	1	0
11. Expresses love by doing things rather than saying.	5	4	3	2	1	0
12. Prefers to follow rather than lead.	5	4	3	2	1	0
13. Is inclined to do tasks with your hands.	5	4	3	2	1	0
14. Prefers not to tell someone "no."	5	4	3	2	1	0
15. Likes having tasks delegated to you.	5	4	3	2	1	0
16. Aims for perfection down to the minute detail.	5	4	3	2	1	0
17. Prefers serving others versus being served.	5	4	3	2	1	0
18. Keeps work area neat and orderly.	5	4	3	2	1	0
19. Is loyal and supportive to those in authority.	5	4	3	2	1	0
20. Finds it difficult to delegate tasks.	5	4	3	2	1	0
COLUMN TOTALS						
TOTAL HANDS PROFILE SCORE						

THINKER LOCATOR™ PROFILE

Draw a circle around the number for each characteristic that best applies to you

BRAIN PROFILE	all the time	most of the time	usually	some of the time	rarely	never
1. Is very methodical in conversation with others.	5	4	3	2	1	0
2. Leans toward being unbiased and objective.	5	4	3	2	1	0
3. Believes reasoning and logic are basis for making decisions.	5	4	3	2	1	0
4. Has a keen intellect.	5	4	3	2	1	0
5. Needs little supervision; is very self-disciplined.	5	4	3	2	1	0
6. Tends to be inquisitive about most things.	5	4	3	2	1	0
7. Is comfortable with having few friends.	5	4	3	2	1	0
8. Dislikes meaningless small talk.	5	4	3	2	1	0
9. Likes researching for solutions to problems.	5	4	3	2	1	0
10. Is cool-headed, in control of emotions.	5	4	3	2	1	0
11. Communicates in a systematic manner.	5	4	3	2	1	0
12. Prefers to read a book than attend a dinner party.	5	4	3	2	1	0
13. Can easily spend hours researching and analyzing info.	5	4	3	2	1	0
14. Is considered neutral and fair in judgment.	5	4	3	2	1	0
15. Feels more at home with one or two friends.	5	4	3	2	1	0
16. Likes conversing with others about intellectual topics.	5	4	3	2	1	0
17. Asks lots of questions.	5	4	3	2	1	0
18. Exercises self-control well.	5	4	3	2	1	0
19. Prefers working with small groups.	5	4	3	2	1	0
20. Backs up opinions with facts and information.	5	4	3	2	1	0

COLUMN TOTALS

TOTAL BRAIN PROFILE SCORE

THINKER LOCATOR™ PROFILE						
Draw a circle around the number for each characteristic that best applies to you						
MOUTH PROFILE	*all the time*	*most of the time*	*usually*	*some of the time*	*rarely*	*never*
1. Is eloquent in speech and communication.	5	4	3	2	1	0
2. Prefers to be with people rather than alone.	5	4	3	2	1	0
3. Instructs and gives advice using step-by-step procedures.	5	4	3	2	1	0
4. Loves to inspire and motivate others.	5	4	3	2	1	0
5. Uses life experiences to validate principles and decisions.	5	4	3	2	1	0
6. Your optimism draws people to you.	5	4	3	2	1	0
7. Analyzes your thoughts when talking to others.	5	4	3	2	1	0
8. Prone to cut off counseling when guidance is not followed.	5	4	3	2	1	0
9. Provides how-to steps on applying guidance.	5	4	3	2	1	0
10. Listens well, but interrupts others to make your point.	5	4	3	2	1	0
11. Has a need to work with people.	5	4	3	2	1	0
12. Shares clear instructions on how to do a task.	5	4	3	2	1	0
13. Memorizes well by saying words aloud.	5	4	3	2	1	0
14. Has a positive "Can Do" attitude.	5	4	3	2	1	0
15. Needs others to bounce ideas and insights off of.	5	4	3	2	1	0
16. Communicates well by showing examples of your life.	5	4	3	2	1	0
17. Needs to quickly settle issues with people.	5	4	3	2	1	0
18. Desires outward, visible feedback from audiences.	5	4	3	2	1	0
19. Enjoys counseling and giving advice.	5	4	3	2	1	0
20. Edifies and encourages people to be their best.	5	4	3	2	1	0
COLUMN TOTALS						
TOTAL MOUTH PROFILE SCORE						

THINKER LOCATOR™ PROFILE						
Draw a circle around the number for each characteristic that best applies to you						
ARMS PROFILE	*all the time*	*most of the time*	*usually*	*some of the time*	*rarely*	*never*
1. Has natural ability to work with finances.	5	4	3	2	1	0
2. Is quick to offer help where there is a need.	5	4	3	2	1	0
3. Loves to give.	5	4	3	2	1	0
4. Had a business as a child.	5	4	3	2	1	0
5. Dislikes wasting resources.	5	4	3	2	1	0
6. Views serving as a privilege.	5	4	3	2	1	0
7. Is diligent in accomplishing goals.	5	4	3	2	1	0
8. Managing business affairs comes easy.	5	4	3	2	1	0
9. Is not easily deceived or duped.	5	4	3	2	1	0
10. Readily gives with no hidden motives.	5	4	3	2	1	0
11. Has an entrepreneurial spirit.	5	4	3	2	1	0
12. Seeks best value and efficiency.	5	4	3	2	1	0
13. Likes fulfilling needs of others.	5	4	3	2	1	0
14. Likes earning lots of money in order to give.	5	4	3	2	1	0
15. Is good at cost cutting.	5	4	3	2	1	0
16. Tends to be frugal in spending on self.	5	4	3	2	1	0
17. Has innate ability for business.	5	4	3	2	1	0
18. Works hard to make money.	5	4	3	2	1	0
19. Enjoys giving secretively.	5	4	3	2	1	0
20. Is steady, industrious in your efforts.	5	4	3	2	1	0
COLUMN TOTALS						
TOTAL ARMS PROFILE SCORE						

THINKER LOCATOR™ PROFILE

Draw a circle around the number for each characteristic that best applies to you

FEET PROFILE	*all the time*	*most of the time*	*usually*	*some of the time*	*rarely*	*never*
1. Is a great organizer of people and resources.	5	4	3	2	1	0
2. Easily sees the big picture behind a situation.	5	4	3	2	1	0
3. Enjoys being in charge.	5	4	3	2	1	0
4. Continuously jots ideas, list reminders to self.	5	4	3	2	1	0
5. Gets satisfaction from completing a difficult project.	5	4	3	2	1	0
6. Leading others comes naturally.	5	4	3	2	1	0
7. Has small amount of knowledge in many areas.	5	4	3	2	1	0
8. Prefers working with people rather than things.	5	4	3	2	1	0
9. Doesn't mind others receiving credit for achieving goals.	5	4	3	2	1	0
10. Likes challenging projects; dislikes mundane tasks.	5	4	3	2	1	0
11. Knows when to initiate change.	5	4	3	2	1	0
12. Is naturally inclined to shoulder accountability.	5	4	3	2	1	0
13. Is interested in the broad view of a situation, not details.	5	4	3	2	1	0
14. Likes using visual aids to explain solutions.	5	4	3	2	1	0
15. Handily administers, organizes, and directs others.	5	4	3	2	1	0
16. Is good at making strategic decisions.	5	4	3	2	1	0
17. Is willing to step up to lead when asked.	5	4	3	2	1	0
18. Is a long-range visionary thinker.	5	4	3	2	1	0
19. Is good at delegating tasks.	5	4	3	2	1	0
20. Takes the initiative to develop projects.	5	4	3	2	1	0
COLUMN TOTALS						
TOTAL FEET PROFILE SCORE						

THINKER LOCATOR™ PROFILE						
Draw a circle around the number for each characteristic that best applies to you						
HEART PROFILE	*all the time*	*most of the time*	*usually*	*some of the time*	*rarely*	*never*
1. Believes most people are good and kind.	5	4	3	2	1	0
2. Has great empathy for those who hurt.	5	4	3	2	1	0
3. Focuses on what is good and right about people.	5	4	3	2	1	0
4. Tends to ignore that a problem exists.	5	4	3	2	1	0
5. Has great compassion for others.	5	4	3	2	1	0
6. Positive and joyful are typical attitudes.	5	4	3	2	1	0
7. Is mindful not to inflict hurt when speaking to others.	5	4	3	2	1	0
8. Tends to operate at a slow pace.	5	4	3	2	1	0
9. Attempts to mend other people's relationships.	5	4	3	2	1	0
10. Often does caring and thoughtful things for others.	5	4	3	2	1	0
11. Does not like dealing with conflict or confrontation.	5	4	3	2	1	0
12. Has an altruistic nature.	5	4	3	2	1	0
13. Is deeply touched by the troubles of other people.	5	4	3	2	1	0
14. Is genuinely happy when good happens for others.	5	4	3	2	1	0
15. Is very trusting of others.	5	4	3	2	1	0
16. Tends to be slow in finishing tasks.	5	4	3	2	1	0
17. Is sensitive to others reactions to your actions.	5	4	3	2	1	0
18. Attempts to solve other people's problems.	5	4	3	2	1	0
19. Stray cats and dogs followed you home as a child.	5	4	3	2	1	0
20. Thinks often about how you can help others.	5	4	3	2	1	0
COLUMN TOTALS						
TOTAL HEART PROFILE SCORE						

THINKER LOCATOR™ PROFILE

Draw a circle around the number for each characteristic that best applies to you

EARS-EYES PROFILE	all the time	most of the time	usually	some of the time	rarely	never
1. Is able to size up people, situations, and circumstances.	5	4	3	2	1	0
2. Has high standard of honesty and integrity.	5	4	3	2	1	0
3. Is very straightforward, direct, and candid in communicating.	5	4	3	2	1	0
4. Can be opinionated.	5	4	3	2	1	0
5. Refuses to perform work at less than excellent.	5	4	3	2	1	0
6. Views situations as either black or white.	5	4	3	2	1	0
7. Works better as an individual or with few people.	5	4	3	2	1	0
8. Is compelling, convincing, and persuasive.	5	4	3	2	1	0
9. Has an intuitive nature.	5	4	3	2	1	0
10. Enjoys being alone.	5	4	3	2	1	0
11. Leans toward perfectionistic behavior.	5	4	3	2	1	0
12. Believes there is never a reason to lie.	5	4	3	2	1	0
13. Prefers to work alone.	5	4	3	2	1	0
14. Is more likely to trust your gut.	5	4	3	2	1	0
15. Stands firmly on your principles.	5	4	3	2	1	0
16. Is good judge of others' character.	5	4	3	2	1	0
17. Has great influence with others.	5	4	3	2	1	0
18. Openly expresses what's on your mind.	5	4	3	2	1	0
19. Perceives when someone is not being truthful.	5	4	3	2	1	0
20. Is inclined to make decisions based on a hunch.	5	4	3	2	1	0
COLUMN TOTALS						
TOTAL EARS-EYES PROFILE SCORE						

THINKER LOCATOR™ PROFILE SCORE CHART	
PROFILE	SCORE
1. HANDS PROFILE	
2. BRAIN PROFILE	
3. MOUTH PROFILE	
4. ARMS PROFILE	
5. FEET PROFILE	
6. HEART PROFILE	
7. EARS-EYES PROFILE	

THINKER LOCATOR™ PROFILE SCORE ANALYSIS

- If one score is much higher than the other profile scores, you have a single profiler thinking work trait (e.g., Feet).

- If you have two scores that are almost the same, you have a double profiler thinking work trait (e.g., Feet-Arms).

- If you have three scores that are similar, you have a triple profiler thinking work trait (e.g., Feet-Arms-Brain).

- If you have four scores that are similar in value, go over your answers again or have a partner review your responses with you to make sure your responses are accurate.

BE YOUR BEST SELF

Now that you have identified your Thinker Locator Profile(s), read about their characteristics. Think about how you can use your profile(s) to re-channel your actions for taking on different tasks or roles in your current work life that will allow you to do what you are motivated to do. Career choices are also listed below each profile. If you are considering taking on a new position, think about which career choices match your talents, abilities, and interests.

Being your best self means being who you are even if nobody else believes in you, supports you, or encourages you. There is no greater gift we can bring to our workplace or to the world than being our best self. When you begin to channel *you* into your work, you will experience one of the greatest joys there is to experience.

THE "HANDS" THINKER LOCATOR PROFILE

Hands are the implementers of the organization. They prefer work that requires the use of their hands. Hands take the policies, instructions, projects, and work orders and turn them into useable products, services, and processes for the customer, clients, and public they serve. They love helping others, so much so that they find it difficult to turn down requests even when their plate is full. Because Hands tend to go beyond the call of duty to complete a project, they expect to be recognized for doing so. Acknowledging them with plaques, certificates, and even just a simple "thank you" will garner them to be more productive.

Mr. Clyde, a mason, takes tremendous pleasure in working his craft with the instruments of his hands. I observed him shape the concrete of my driveway like a sculptor shapes a sculpture. When the concrete was poured, he took the time to methodically ensure every corner was completely filled. After Mr. Clyde leveled the driveway, he got down on his hands and knees to inspect every inch, searching for gaps and cracks. He finished up by shaping each side in a unique design that represented his brand and imprint.

Hands prefer to follow the leaders in the organization rather than being leaders. They are some of the most supportive and loyal people to their leaders and organizations. If you have a project that requires attention to detail, give it to Hands. Just make sure the project is broken into small components that can be completed in a short period of time. Hands can get overwhelmed if their share of a job involves working for the long haul.

CAREER CHOICES FOR THE "HANDS" PROFILE

- administrative assistant
- airline/auto mechanic
- architect
- assembly worker
- auditor
- bookkeeper/accountant
- builder
- bus/truck driver
- carpenter
- cashier
- clerk
- computer operator
- computer programmer
- computer technician
- cook
- copyeditor
- craftsman
- crane operator
- custodian
- dock worker
- dog/baby sitter
- electrician
- farmer
- farm worker
- fire person
- fisherman
- flight attendant
- food preparer
- forest ranger
- game designer
- geographer
- government worker
- graphic designer

- health care technician
- home health care aide
- hostler
- hygienist
- industrial designer
- interior designer
- landscaper
- librarian
- limo driver
- maid
- mason
- mathematician
- meteorologist
- miner
- nanny
- nurse
- pet groomer
- plumber
- postman
- radiologist
- receptionist
- repair person
- seamstress
- shipbuilder
- textile presser
- ticket taker
- toolmaker
- waiter/waitress
- website designer
- X-ray technician
- zookeeper
- zoologist

THE "BRAIN" THINKER LOCATOR PROFILE

The Brain profile is naturally inquisitive. This profile wants to be "in the know." That's why they spend lots of time reading, researching, and studying knowledge in all areas, but especially in their area of expertise. They stay abreast of industry and market trends that can affect the viability of their organization. When an associate recommends a different or innovative system or approach, the Brain fires back with questions: *how, why, what, where,* and *when?* They believe decisions must be validated with facts, research, and/or statistics, making for a more unbiased objective decision. Brains are the checks-and-balances of the organization. They're considered the analytical know-it-all.

Brains also love to enlighten, teach, train, and tutor others in a systematic way the things they have learned. Want to learn how to become self-disciplined? Hang around a Brain. They know how to stay on purpose in achieving their goals. The Brain is also the calm profile, able to maintain control of their emotions.

Jack Shaughnessy, a licensed real estate broker enjoys training real estate agents. Because he spends a lot of time researching the real estate industry and keeping abreast of the laws and trends, he is looked upon by his colleagues as the office expert. Jack even forewarned his agents of the real estate meltdown long before it occurred. Many agents paid heed to his warnings by making adjustments, while others did not.

CAREER CHOICES FOR THE "BRAIN" PROFILE

- actuarial scientist
- anesthesiologist
- anthropologist
- archaeologist
- astronomer
- author (nonfiction)
- biologist
- business analyst
- chemist
- chiropractor
- clergy
- college professor
- composer
- computer analyst/ programmer
- coroner
- curator
- doctor of philosophy
- engineer
- geologist
- journalist
- judge
- librarian
- market researcher
- medical technician
- meteorologist
- nutritionist
- oceanographer
- pharmacist
- physician
- physicist
- playwright
- research scientist
- science technician
- statistician
- surgeon general
- teacher
- television/newspaper reporter
- therapist
- trainer

THE "MOUTH" THINKER LOCATOR PROFILE

While most of the other profiles think internally, Mouths think out loud. When Mouths tell people what they are thinking, they are actually brainstorming. Sometimes, they have a notepad handy to record what they hear from their mind.

The Mouth profile uses its mouth to inspire, urge, cheer, stimulate, support, and motivate others. Mouths keep the rhythm of optimism flowing in their teams and organizations. They love to influence others to raise their skill proficiency. That's why they prefer working with people rather than with things. They notice when co-workers are getting off track and step in with encouragement to redirect them. That's what Tumika Pierce, a senior case support technician at the Social Security Administration, did. She helped workers stay on track when the agency had a hiring freeze. Everybody was on overload with having to do more work with fewer people. As a result, morale was low. Tumika encouraged her co-workers through her infectious spirit. She would recognize each person's birthday by having a party for them in the office. Once she brought in her video camera to record co-workers in action on the job. She then used the recordings to create a skit highlighting "Social Security Workers in the Broadcast News." No matter how bad things got, she always had a positive word to share. Tumika's actions instilled pride, value, and camaraderie in the office during a difficult time.

The Mouth Thinker Locator Profile brings a lightness of spirit to the organization, always focusing on the bright side of things. They often serve as the spokesperson for the team or organization. Mouths get so excited about giving practical step-by-step advice to help others that they will sometimes cut off other people's thoughts before the person is able to finish saying them. Mouths are often adamant that their advice be put into action by the recipients. When it is not, they may sever the relationship.

CAREER CHOICES FOR THE "MOUTH" PROFILE

- administrative assistant
- advertising account executive
- auctioneer
- clergy/pastor
- coach
- customer service rep.
- diplomat
- disc jockey
- human resources manager
- motivational speaker
- psychologist
- public relations manager
- real estate agent
- receptionist
- recreation director
- school counselor
- social worker
- speech therapist
- television anchor person
- television announcer
- ticket/reservation agent
- travel agent

THE "ARMS" THINKER LOCATOR PROFILE

The expression "He has his arms wide open to give" perfectly describes the Arms profile. This profile loves contributing to others' lives in meaningful ways. They especially enjoy giving secretively. If you find a gift on your desk or a deed that was done without a note, it was probably an Arms who did it.

Richard Hardon, an entrepreneur in the oil business, wakes up in the morning with thoughts of who he can give to today. It's his M.O., mode of operation. One of his favorite ways of giving is distributing thousands of books and CDs that inspire and teach people how to fulfill their highest potential.

Working with numbers and money also comes easy for Arms. They seek efficiency and best value for their workplace. Arms dislike waste of the organization's resources, especially time and money. Keeping a check-and- balance on the company spending, they prevent associates from overspending. Arms are excellent at cost-cutting and maximizing profits in retrenching their organizations. Their primary motive for working hard to make money is to be able to give more. Although Arms live to give, they are not easily manipulated into giving to people and organizations with unscrupulous motives. They tend to be frugal in spending on themselves.

CAREER CHOICES FOR THE "ARMS" PROFILE

- accountant
- actor
- auditor
- banker
- bank teller
- bookkeeper
- broker
- business coach
- business consultant
- business teacher
- contractor
- custodian
- economist
- entrepreneur
- evangelist
- farmer
- investment fund manager
- manufacturer
- missionary
- paramedic
- purchasing agent
- retailer
- salesperson

THE "FEET" THINKER LOCATOR PROFILE

The feet are the first body part in action; they lead the body. When standing, feet take on the entire weight of the body. In an organization, Feet operate in a similar fashion. They are the forerunners, team leaders, organizers, and administrators who assume and uphold accountability for the organization. Feet point in one direction and the entire organization or department follows. They have Big Picture thinking; they're the visionaries of the company.

Larry Doty, sales manager for the Del Monte Company, inherited the worst sales region in the country for the company. The region had not met its sales goals for the previous eight years. Larry didn't allow that to bother him. In fact, it was a challenge he welcomed. He began by taking each salesperson out one-on-one and getting their input on solutions. Then he engaged the company's customers as well. Based on these two constituents, Larry put together a plan for the region to become #1 in the country. Because he had sought their input, the salespeople embraced the strategy and followed his direction. Enthusiasm was at an all-time high. Exactly one year after implementing Larry's new strategy, his team became the #1 region in the country.

The Feet profile has the ability to achieve goals and tasks by organizing people and resources for a common good. The passion and excitement Feet have for the vision/ mission of the team and/or organization comes naturally. Feet like being in control, but are able to submit to the authority of others in order to have their own authority over a particular domain. Generally, Feet are bombarded with ideas and insights, which they are constantly jotting down on Post-it notes, pads, and BlackBerrys. Feet love challenging assignments and are able to persist over the long haul in getting them accomplished. Sometimes they tend to allow their zeal for work to infringe on their personal life, causing them to neglect their relationships.

CAREER CHOICES FOR THE "FEET" PROFILE

- advertising executive
- airline pilot
- athletic coach
- attorney
- city planner
- clergy/pastor
- contractor
- department store manager
- diplomat
- distributor
- entrepreneur
- hospital administrator
- hotel manager
- human resources manager
- judge
- marketing executive
- military officer
- natural science manager
- news director
- politician
- product brand manager
- public administrator
- public relations director
- publisher
- radio/TV producer
- restaurant manager
- salesperson
- school principal
- senior planner

THE "HEART" THINKER LOCATOR PROFILE

People who are the "heart" of the organization, and thus the Heart profile, think with their heart, not with their head. They think about the customer, client, patient, or public. They are more concerned with other people's needs than their own, especially those who are hurting. They are not in the WIIFM ("What's in it for me?") crowd. They are in the WIIFY ("What's in it for you?") crowd. They wake up with WIIFY on their mind.

Customers love Hearts, because they truly care about giving their customers the best service and go the extra mile to do so. In a commodity-driven business environment, where there is little distinction between comparative products, a Heart can be a company's best competitive advantage. Hearts create satisfied loyal customers who return to your business even when your competitor is more economical for them. Hearts, whether working as a graphic designer or a science teacher, are motivated by what their work is doing for others. Melissa Benedict, for example, a research scientist at the Nathan S. Kline Institute for Psychiatric Research, is motivated by helping others. She says, "If we can help just one person with the research we're doing, that's really rewarding. Hopefully it will help people in the long run."

On the other hand, Hearts avoid conflict and confrontation; hence, they are not prompt to handle problems or controversial issues. Because Hearts are trusting and ready to believe the best about people, they can be gullible in making decisions. They are quick to celebrate when good things happen for others.

CAREER CHOICES FOR THE "HEART" PROFILE

- artist
- art teacher
- career counselor
- commercial artist
- composer
- drama teacher
- environmentalist
- event planner
- groomer
- home economist
- home health care aide
- homemaker
- interior decorator
- kindergarten teacher
- massage therapist
- model
- musician
- music teacher
- nurse
- nursery teacher
- nutritionist
- occupational therapist
- office worker
- performing artist
- personal coach
- photographer
- physical therapist
- social worker
- special education teacher
- veterinarian
- welfare worker
- zookeeper
- zoologist

"EARS-EYES" THINKER LOCATOR PROFILE

Ears-Eyes are the hearers and seers of the organization. They have foresight, a keen sense of awareness, intuition, and perception, which is used to constantly evaluate, analyze, assess, and judge the elements of their workplace. Ears-Eyes have the uncanny ability to take a look at a new initiative and point out a clear, decisive direction, "Let's start looking at A, C, and E, but not B and D. We don't want to get caught in a short-term flop." Generally, they are on target. What bothers some on the team is that because Ears-Eyes work from intuition, they often can't substantiate their suggestions with hard facts. In spite of facing criticism from colleagues, they are willing to make tough, unpopular suggestions and decisions. They trust their ability to grasp and comprehend that which is obscure to everyone else. It's said they have hearing and insight that go beyond the obvious.

Kimberly Davis had tremendous insight when Chase Manhattan, Chemical Bank, and Manufacturer's Hanover merged. The corporate cultures of these three institutions were clashing, causing mistrust, frustration, and resentment among employees. Davis was working with Chase in a P&L (profit-and-loss) position when she received a call from the head of Human Resources. He offered her a two-year position in his department. Colleagues felt it would be a mistake for her to leave P&L, but her keen insight and perception overruled and she took the job. It paid off. Davis said, "It was a wonderful way to learn the new organization from the top. I was able to see all of the businesses as opposed to being in the one narrow business pre-merger." She emerged from the merger as senior vice president of Global Philanthropy at JPMorganChase and president of the JPMorganChase Foundation.

Ears-Eyes are very good at persuading others their way too. They have sound judgment and are quick on their feet. They see things in black and white; there are no gray areas. It's either right or wrong.

CAREER CHOICES FOR THE "EYES-EARS" PROFILE

- actuarial scientist
- airline pilot
- air traffic controller
- art critic
- attorney
- clergy
- consultant
- coroner
- crime investigator
- diplomat
- editorialist
- inspector general
- insurance underwriter
- judge
- market researcher
- military officer
- navigator
- newspaper/TV critic
- news reporter
- paramedic
- philosopher
- police officer
- program evaluator
- quality controller
- science teacher
- science technician
- systems analyst
- theologian

EMPOWERMENT THOUGHTS

- I have unique intrinsic value that is different from anyone else, which I use to benefit my employer, co-workers, staff, clients, and associates.

- I will take time to reflect on how to best direct my Thinker Locator Profile so that it lines up with my interests as well as my skills, abilities, and talents.

- I will be patient with my efforts as I rethink my Thinker to be my best self. I realize that it may take time before I experience the results I want in my work life.

- I accept that others may not like the authentic me, and I am okay with that. I will not allow others non approval to keep me from being true to myself.

To receive your free in-depth
Empowerment Thought,
log on to www.ciemurray.com.

Empowerment Tool of the Chooser
Making the Right Moves

*"The greater part of our happiness or misery depends
on our dispositions and not our circumstances."*
—MARTHA WASHINGTON

HAPPINESS IS A CHOICE. I didn't want to believe this statement when I first heard it several years ago from Sam. Sam and I were working in an environment where we didn't like the boss. We hated the office politics, the long hours, and the city we were living in. And yet while Sam was happy, I was miserable. Why was Sam happy but I wasn't? Because of the Choosers I was choosing. As Abraham Lincoln once said, "Most people are about as happy as they make up their minds to be." The Empowerment Tool of the Chooser is: *the moves we make in life.* Some moves empower us to be happy, productive, and successful at work. Others disempower us to be unhappy, unproductive, and unsuccessful.

What kind of Choosers are you making? Before deciding to do something at work, stop and think about

The Empowerment Tool of the Chooser is: **the moves we make in life**.

the consequences of your Chooser. Choosers are like playing a game of chess—your boss or co-worker makes a certain move that rubs you the wrong way, and now it's your move. In chess, whatever move you make will impact the move your partner-player makes, ultimately determining whether you win or lose the game. And so it is in your workplace; whatever Chooser you decide will impact your staff, co-workers, or boss's next move, ultimately determining whether you win or lose in the situation. But instead of winning or losing your queen in chess, you could lose the other's trust, confidence, the relationship, special project, promotion, raise, or job. And while you can't control the moves somebody else makes, you can control yours to win the game.

Let's take a look at three real work situations and observe the Choosers Amy, Jonathan, and Frank made.

VICTIM OR VICTOR

Amy loves her job but feels she is a victim of John, her toxic, micro-managing boss. He constantly checks up on her and seems to enjoy pitting her against her co-workers. John is known for his outbursts, screams, and obscenities with his entire staff. What irks Amy most is the makeshift projects he assigns her that eat into her productivity.

Most micro-managers are driven by fear and a lack of trust within themselves that leads them to want to do checks-and-balances on everything everyone else does. The key in this circumstance is to recognize that it's not about you; it's about them needing to control the situation so that their worst fears do not come true. They are acting out of a Thinker (thoughts of the heart and head) based in fear, rather than one based in confidence. Perhaps they have performance demands for their department and instead of thinking, "We can do it," they focus on what will happen if their team or staff doesn't pull it off. As a result, they operate in a state of panic, and most times don't realize their behavior is producing exactly what they are trying to avoid. They become what I call "brutal aggressors." Think about it with this analogy: When some parents have fearful thoughts about bodily harm coming to a child, their response is to react with brutal aggression. It's the same motivation here.

Given that reality, what moves can Amy make to keep from being sucked into her boss's toxic ways? Well, she can learn to detach from John's behavior. First, she has to realize that *it's not about her* and that she should not allow John to get her emotionally involved in his insecurities and fear. How can she do that? It's true that what John says and does is cruel. But it's also true that nothing that happens outside of us can hurt us, unless we give it permission to. What other people do and don't do is not our problem. It's *their* problem.

...nothing that happens outside of us can hurt us, unless we give it permission to.

Next, Amy needs to refuse to pass John's brutal aggression on to others. You too must refuse to allow others' behavior to throw you off from what you would normally do in the workplace. Don't allow others' actions to hijack your day. If this behavior is regular and consistent for John, Amy could create a plan for counteracting it—proactively choosing healthy behaviors that will take care of her emotional well-being when she is at work.

In addition, Amy could pray for John and his well-being. Why should she do that for someone so offensive? Actually the prayer will do more for Amy than it will likely do for John. She will find that she is much more able to detach herself from him and release the hold his tyrant behavior has had on her.

PAUSE OR RASH

Make Choosers that will protect your future rather than your feelings. To do this you have to resist getting even with the person who falsely accused or back-stabbed you. Any move you make while being in an emotional state is usually the wrong move.

Be on the alert for hurt feelings, which can cause you to make distorted decisions.

My friend Jonathan got offended when his boss accused him of cheating on his expense report. He was so full of rage that he quit his job on the spot, not thinking about his non-working pregnant wife and financial obligations at home. It took him eight months to find a comparable job.

Jonathan didn't protect his future; he allowed his hurt to take control. Like Jonathan, we all have been or will get hurt by someone somewhere along the line. While it is important to acknowledge the hurt feelings, that doesn't mean we need to allow the feelings to take charge. Be on the alert for hurt feelings, because they can lead you to lose perspective of the situation, which can cause you to make distorted decisions. Step back and ask yourself, "How would I handle this situation if I were not having unpleasant feelings like hurt, anger, resentment?" Coach yourself to respond to the situation as if you were having pleasant feelings like calmness and serenity.

BITTER OR BETTER

Frank, a project manager for an accounting firm, was under a time crunch for a project. He was highly admired within the firm because of his congenial personality. He went up to his assistant, Flora, who was on the phone at her desk. He stood there for a minute, hoping to get her attention. When she didn't look up, he patted her on the shoulder. Flora then put the person on hold and Frank gave her a task he needed to have done immediately. Frank thought nothing more of the incident until he received a copy of an email Flora had sent to his boss accusing him of hitting her and knocking her shoulder out of whack. Frank was in absolute disbelief that Flora could exaggerate the situation this way.

The discord between them began to affect Frank's attitude and began to trickle down to his work. He attempted to talk with her about it, but she refused to admit that she had done anything wrong. Tired of carrying around anger that was now turning into resentment, Frank decided one day to make amends with her. He said, "Flora, if I said or did anything to offend you, I apologize." Flora suddenly began to cry. She never admitted her role in the discord nor did she apologize. Because Frank took the high road to end the conflict, he brought harmony back to his work environment.

HOW TO MAKE CHOOSERS

At this point, you may be thinking, "Cie, I don't work at any of those industries and the situations don't apply to my work environment. How am I to know what moves to make at my company with the situation I am facing?" To answer that question, I have provided my "10 Commandments of Workplace Empowerment" as a guideline to help steer you in selecting the appropriate Chooser. Choosing to do these commandments will make for a happier workplace for you, your co-workers, bosses, and employees.

10 COMMANDMENTS FOR WORKPLACE EMPOWERMENT

#1 RESPECT YOURSELF

Respect and honor your boss and co-workers, even if you think they don't deserve it. Recognize and acknowledge them when they do something well, not just when they do something wrong. Try to put yourself in their shoes. When you respect others, they will respect you.

#2 PAUSE

Refuse to make a rash decision when you are emotionally charged with anger and resentment. Hold off for the air to clear, so you can get a better perspective. Major decisions like quitting your job, asking for a transfer, and going over your boss's head should be delayed until your emotions have subsided. The move you make when you are angry is generally not the same one you'd make when you are not.

#3 JUST SAY "NO"

One of the most unkind things you can do is to tell someone "yes" when you really mean "no." Why? Because your heart is not in the "yes." The "no" shows up anyway when you do a half-baked job on the project, miss the deadline you promised, or just don't do what you said "yes" to. Let your "no" be "no" and your "yes" be "yes." Your talk is cheap unless your behavior matches it. If you don't want to do something just say "no." When you say "yes," then do it!

#4 ADMIT IT

Be willing to admit that you messed up. Everybody makes mistakes. There is no shame in making a mistake. The key is to learn from it. Thomas Edison, when discussing his many attempts at inventing the light bulb, said, "I have not failed. I've just found 10,000 ways that won't work."

#5 MIND YOUR OWN BUSINESS

Keep your nose out of other people's business. Live your life, do your job, and let others do theirs.

#6 SERVE

Look to see how you can help others and your organization, rather than how your organization can help you. Don't refuse to do a task just because it's outside of your job description or your Thinker Locator Profile. Take ownership of your work environment.

#7 HOLD NO GRUDGES

Resist trying to get even with a co-worker, boss, or employee who hurt you by taking action that will cause the person harm. Refuse to let them get the best of you by walking around with a chip on your shoulder. Some people don't know that their behavior was perceived as being rude, abrasive, inconsiderate, or uncouth. Just say to yourself, "He must be having a bad day. I'm not going to have a bad one with him." If you feel the need to express your feelings, wait until your emotions have cooled. Make up your mind to forgive them, even if for no other reason than to keep from punishing yourself with the negative feelings you'd otherwise be carrying around over them.

#8 ACCEPT REALITY

Accept that change, the unexpected, and conflict are not bad things that are "happening to you." They are a part of life. Deal with the conflict, stay flexible for the unexpected, and embrace change. The sooner you can move into accepting the reality of the situation, the quicker you'll be able to determine a solution.

#9 DO UNTO OTHERS

Do unto others as you want them to do unto you. If you don't want others to gossip, lie, backstab, or use name-calling or profanity toward you, then don't gossip, lie, backstab, or use name-calling or profanity toward others.

#10 RESIST COMPETITIVE JEALOUSY

Seek to beat *your* best performance, not your co-worker's. Congratulate others when they sell a new client or get a promotion. When you do this, you are getting closer to your own breakthrough.

BEFORE YOU QUIT, TRY THIS

Quitting is a drastic move you may not need to make to create the engaging, fulfilling, successful work life you desire. So, before you quit, consider *repositioning* yourself where you are. Explore what opportunities are in your current workplace that would enhance your work life. What new tasks and assignments could you take on? Seek tasks that fit your interests and your Thinker Locator Profile while increasing your skills, value, and marketability. For instance, if most of the tasks you are doing are outside of your Thinker Locator Profile, offer to help co-workers complete some of their tasks that fit your profile. If your primary profile is Feet, but your job contains a lot of tasks for Hands, help your co-worker with some of his organizational responsibilities. Go to your manager and volunteer for temporary and short-term assignments that will expand your profile experience. These short-term roles can also provide an opportunity for you to determine whether you'll enjoy this type of work and even expose you to working with different people within the organization.

...before you quit, consider **repositioning** *yourself where you are.*

Finally, seek opportunities outside of the office—at professional associations or at non-profit, social, religious, and community organizations. You will surely find many roles to be filled that will be rewarding and provide the sense of accomplishment you are longing for.

IS IT TIME TO LEAVE?

Sometimes the move you need to make *is* to another workplace. But, as I've said, make sure that you're not running from something that can be alleviated by volunteering for a different set of responsibilities or by a change in your attitude. For, if you don't gain a proper perspective and resolve it where you are, you will likely find yourself dealing with a similar or worse situation in your next workplace.

How do you know when it's time to leave? Perhaps you are in the wrong kind of work. I have a friend who is a miserable, unsuccessful lawyer who would be a happy, successful electrician. He hesitates to make the move because he deems being a professional more important than doing fulfilling work. Other factors for leaving are inadequate pay, unethical activity, toxic relationships with superiors, and a mismatch of cultures.

Debra Davenport, Ph.D., president of DavenportFolio, has developed an assessment tool to help you decide on whether to seek a different workplace. It only takes a couple of minutes to complete. The instructions are on the next page.

ASSESS YOURSELF

Check the statements that apply to you and ignore for now the letter after each statement.

1. I look forward to going to work most every day. (S)

2. My employer treats me fairly and with respect. (S)

3. I live for the weekend, or any days away from work. (G)

4. I feel valued and appreciated for my professional contributions. (S)

5. My workplace feels "toxic." (G)

6. I can be myself at work and not have to worry about being judged. (S)

7. I am included in my company's "information loop." (S)

8. My employer discusses with me and provides opportunities for advancement and professional development. (S)

9. I am commended for the extra effort I perform. (S)

10. I am stimulated intellectually and creatively by my work. (S)

11. I feel that I am making a positive contribution to society. (S)

12. I am compensated well for my work. (S)

13. I find myself daydreaming frequently about a new career. (G)

14. I feel that my work is a natural extension of who I am as a human being. (S)

15. I see myself as successful. (S)

16. I feel trapped and stuck in my current position. (G)

17. I feel in control of my career destiny. (S)

18. I am working at the level of my full potential. (S)

19. My current career negatively impacts those close to me. (G)

20. I have a desire to try something new and different. (G)

Now, count the number of "S" and "G" responses you have. "S" means "Stay" and "G" means "Go."

This checklist is a reliable indicator of whether or not your present job is a good fit for you. Clearly, the more "G" ("Go") responses you checked, the more critical it is for you to start thinking about new opportunities.

EMPOWERMENT THOUGHTS

- Before I make a move, I will stop and think about the consequences of my Choosers.

- Just because someone is moody, accusatory, inconsiderate, or is having a bad day doesn't mean I have to be moody, accusatory, inconsiderate, or have a bad day.

- I admit when I'm wrong or make a mistake. I strive to learn from my mistakes.

- I accept that change, conflict, and confrontation are sometimes a part of my work life. I choose to look at these as opportunities to learn, grow, and develop into being my best self.

To receive your free in-depth
Empowerment Thought,
log on to www.ciemurray.com.

Empowerment Tool of the Sayer
Empower Yourself

"The power of your own words leads you to greatness."
—KEITH HARRELL

CHARLES MURRAY WAS A FRESHMAN in college when he was recruited by the Southwestern Publishing Company to sell books door-to-door during the upcoming summer break. He was excited about the opportunity this job posed for him, but first he had to convince his mom to allow him to go. Her answer was an emphatic "no"! "You would be moving 1,000 miles from home, living with people we don't know." It didn't matter what Charles said to reassure her, her answer remained the same. Getting desperate, Charles asked his Aunt Carrie to intercede for him. Aunt Carrie told Charles, "Don't worry, you will go to Cleveland, Ohio, this summer."

Charles did go to Cleveland that summer and then to five different cities over the next five summers, earning money to pay for his schooling all the way through law school. Every morning before Charles would leave the

The Empowerment Tool of the Sayer is telling yourself what you want to have.

house to make his sales calls, he would build himself up with the declarations that Southwestern had given him. He'd say things like, "I feel healthy. I feel terrific. I feel outstanding." He would then say this to himself throughout the day. More than 20 years later, Charles still creates a work vision for himself with his words.

EMPOWER YOURSELF

Have you heard the saying, "Actions speak louder than words"? While this saying has great impact, it's undeniable that it's our *words* that move us to *action*. What was Charles doing each morning? He was using his words to empower himself into action to obtain what he wanted. The Empowerment Tool of the Sayer is telling yourself what you want to have. So many times we use words to talk ourselves into having what we don't want instead of using words to talk ourselves into having what we do want. In the movie *Remember the Titans*, starring Denzel Washington, two opposing high school football teams are united as one team due to racial integration of the two schools. The teams initially struggle to become a united team during football camp. One of the things that helps them to unite is the Sayer tool. They use the tool to establish the vision for what they want to have. When they come out on the football field for their games, each player sings the words, "We are the Titans, the Mighty Mighty Titans. We're good, we're real good. You'll remember the night you played the Titans." They become mighty alright, winning that game and finishing the season 13-0 in the state championship.

What have you been saying about your work life? Is it, "This place makes me sick. I hate my job, my boss, and co-workers"? If so, then hating your job is the reality you are no doubt getting. If you don't want what you've been saying, then begin saying what you do want. How about, "I have a work life that empowers me to be my best self"? After all, it's your Sayer tool that guides your Thinker, and your Thinker that influences your actions.

Let's say you've just been given a challenging project with a tight deadline. Instead of getting anxious and telling yourself, "This is hard. I don't think I can finish it on time," start telling yourself, "It's a piece of cake" or "I know this project will become easy."

HOW DOES THE SAYER TOOL WORK?

I've heard it said that "the way you hear yourself is not the same as how you hear from others." You have an outer ear and

...what you say to yourself is more powerful than what others say to you.

an inner ear. When you speak out loud to yourself, your inner ear recognizes your voice, picks it up, and feeds your voice directly to your heart. Remember the first time you recorded your voice and played it back? The recorded voice is the one everybody else hears. But the voice you hear sounds different, and it's the one your inner ear recognizes. Medical science describes the inner ear as that part of the brain that controls your speech. It is connected to every nerve in your body. Medical science also concludes that the words you speak can even affect your health. When you use your Sayer, you are actually planting words in your heart. That's why what you say to yourself is more powerful than what others say to you.

Am I saying that you can replace negative thoughts by saying positive words? Yes, it's that simple. I'll prove it to you. Do this little exercise: Start counting from 1 to 10 silently to yourself. When you're at 5, say your name out loud. What happened?... If you did the exercise, you probably noticed that the counting stopped. Similarly, when you begin to speak words aloud that are positive, you invariably stop your negative thoughts.

CAVEAT: YOUR THINKER DOESN'T LIKE CHANGE

When you begin to say new words, your Thinker will resist them. It will tell you "no," by shouting even more discouraging thoughts at you. Be gentle with your Thinker. Tell it, "Okay, I know you've thought that way for a long time, but now we're rethinking our Thinker."

POWER-UP YOURSELF

Whether times are good or times are bad does not have to control the results you get in the world. It's the words that come out of your mouth that can redirect the outcomes of your work life. When you say a word, you're actually saying a thing. For instance, when you say "dog," you don't necessary see the letters "d-o-g"; you see a picture or an image in your mind of an animal called a "dog." When you say, "I can make that sale," it isn't the words themselves that you are seeing. You see a vision or picture of yourself with a prospect, closing a deal. Conversely, when you say, "I can't make that sale," you see an image of yourself at a presentation with a prospect having not made a sale. What type of Sayers have you been saying?

THREE SAYER TYPES

There are three types of Sayers: disempowering, empowering, and neutral. Let's take a look at the Disempowering Sayer. Disempowering Sayers are phrases that focus on a problem you don't want. For instance, you go to the break room and strike up a conversation with a co-worker. You both begin to talk about the pending merger between your firm and a larger conglomerate. You say, "I heard that 1,500 people will be laid off. I'm so worried that I'll be one of them." You begin to get a vision of failure, even though it's not what you want. You start thinking about it. Then that thinking turns into worry, and fear sets in. You now actually believe that what you fear is going to happen, so, without realizing it, you kick into action to start making failure happen. You start coming in late, and your work gets sloppy. You get laid off and say, "I knew this was going to happen!" Instead of talking yourself into obtaining the problem, reverse your words and start talking yourself into achieving the solution.

The second type of Sayer is the Empowering Sayer. This Sayer talks about the solution rather than the problem. You meet up with a different co-worker in the break room and the conversation is about the merger. Your co-worker asks, "Did you hear about the merger? I understand 1,500 people are going to be laid off." You respond by paraphrasing a quote from Walt Disney, "Some people are licked if they can't get a job, but I figure there is always something I can do should jobs become scarce."

Later, you get a vision of your work life and start thinking and believing that it's successful. You start moving into action, identifying growth opportunities, knocking on doors to get to know people at the new company. You're not participating in the fear like your co-workers are; you're taking control of your destiny. You don't mind that your job was eliminated, because you were offered an even better job.

The final Sayer is the Neutral Sayer. These are generally meaningless phrases that do not impact your work outcomes. Small talk about the weather and what you did over the weekend are some examples.

POWER-UP OTHERS

Recently I watched an episode of the television show *I Love Lucy*. Lucy, her husband Ricky, and their friends Fred and Ethel were preparing to play a game of bridge. But no one wanted to be Lucy's partner. They told her she was a terrible bridge player. They also asked her not to tell any more of her lousy jokes. Lucy took their comments to heart and began to feel bad about herself to the point that she got depressed and stayed in bed all day. Her husband and friends realized the impact their negative words had on her, so they told her that they didn't mean it. But Lucy didn't believe them.

One day Ricky got the idea that if telling Lucy negative words had impacted her behavior negatively, then perhaps telling her the opposite would have an opposite effect. When Lucy told a bad joke, they laughed. They told her that she was a great jokester. Now when they got ready to play bridge, they fought over who would be her partner. They told her they all wanted to play with her because she was so good at playing bridge. It worked. Lucy's demeanor changed from depressed to happy.

I'm not advocating being dishonest with your associates. Even as a leader, there are times you will need to chasten an employee in an area of their work or misconduct. However, the delivery of your message can be done in a manner that leaves them encouraged. It takes no more effort to use encouraging Sayers than it does to use discouraging ones. Discouraging, demoralizing, defeatist words can cause a person to have a defeatist attitude; whereas positive, encouraging words can inspire someone to win in life. Make a decision to encourage your employees, your co-workers, your clients, and your boss. Yes, your boss! Your boss is human and needs encouragement too. You will be amazed at the impact this tool will have on your work life.

CREATE A NEW VISION OF YOUR WORK LIFE

What is your vision for yourself at work? In other words, what do you want? To get what you want, you've first got to claim what you want. Otherwise, you can end up with what you don't want. To create a vision of what you want, assess your current work life. Then list both what you don't like or want and what you do want. Use the Work Vision Table below to assist you.

WORK VISION TABLE

	Describe Current Work Life	Describe What You Don't Want	Describe What You Want
Type of Work Tasks			
Work Culture			
Position/Title			
Work Values (e.g., life balance, vacation, flex time, etc.)			

A vision statement is a one to two sentence statement that summarizes the things you want in the workplace. Create your vision statement utilizing the wants you listed in the vision table. Write down your vision statement below. Copy and paste it in a place that you can readily see it, and read it out loud every day.

_____

_____

_____

_____

_____

_____

_____

_____

Now that you have a vision of what you want, make a plan to obtain what you want. After all, what good is a vision or goal without a plan? What good is a plan if you don't take action? One of the major reasons most people don't get the work life they want is because they lack a plan for getting it.

VISION ACTION PLAN

Vision Statement:

_____

_____

_____

_____

_____

_____

_____

_____

_____

Short-Term Steps (1 Year or Less):

_____

_____

_____

_____

_____

Sub-steps:

_____

_____

_____

_____

_____

_____

Long-Term Steps (1 Year or Greater):

_____

_____

_____

_____

_____

Sub-steps:

_____

_____

_____

_____

_____

EMPOWERMENT THOUGHTS

- Instead of talking myself out of obtaining what I want, I will talk myself into having what I want.

- It is hard to empower someone else until I've empowered myself. I will take at least five minutes each morning to empower myself.

- I have a vision of the right work for me. I enjoy the recognition, fulfillment, and health that my right work provides.

- I take the necessary action toward accomplishing my work vision.

To receive your free in-depth
Empowerment Thought,
log on to www.ciemurray.com.

CHAPTER 5

Empowerment Tool of the Player
Turning Work into Play

"Work is the highest form of play."
—AUTHOR UNKNOWN

REMEMBER WHEN I WAS AROUND five years old, my mom would order me and my brothers, Paul and Henry, to go outside to play. My favorite play activity was building sand castles and dungeons in the sand box. We didn't have a sand box at home, but our church, located across the street, had one. My brothers would help me scoop the sand into big piles. Then we would start on the design of the castle. I would gather Popsicle sticks to build a bridge, while Henry would find a container to bring water to fill up the moat. I loved it because I could just let my imagination flow. If I didn't like the way the castle was turning out, I could just knock it down and start over. Little did I know I was learning how to play at work.

The Empowerment Tool of the Player is not just about forming a hobby, playing a game, or spending time with friends. It is about incorporating the experience of play in

The Empowerment Tool of the Player is not just about forming a hobby, it is about incorporating the experience of play in your work.

your work. When we play—whether at our work or in our personal lives—we are keeping the rhythm of joy flowing inside us.

What was I learning while building my sand castles? I learned to work in a cooperative manner as a team. When my brothers wanted to include something I didn't like, I learned that throwing a temper tantrum while kicking the castle over didn't work—because then they no longer wanted to play with me. I also discovered that when I built a castle alone, it was not as much fun or as grand as the ones we built together. Without realizing it, I was learning to control my emotions and how to better work with others.

All of us participated in play activities as children. What kinds of play activities did you do? What was it exactly that we were doing when engaged in play? We were connecting with others. We were also processing fear, anger, worry; we were taking risks, thinking in the moment, being spontaneous, exploring objections, being curious, solving problems, and even dealing with pressure. Play was showing us how to live life joyously.

WHAT HAPPENED TO OUR PLAY?

Even educators know that children learn better when play is involved. Drop in on any nursery, kindergarten, or first- or second-grade class and you'll notice that most of the instructing is done through play. In school, play is synonymous with work. This is because, according to the National Institute for Play (NIFP), kids' knowledge base is enlarged faster with play. However, as children get older, the play activities begin to get separated from the work activities of learning. Then play gets relegated to the playground or afterschool activities.

And so it is with most workplaces; adults do not play at work. Most adults save playing for the weekend or vacation. I, too, used to push my play to the weekend, vacations, and sometimes to the evening hours. But when I started my marketing consulting business, I stopped playing even during non-work hours. My job required innovation, creativity, new ideas, concepts, and solutions for my clients. I now spent almost all of my time focused on work. And yet part of me knew that, by not playing anymore, I was neglecting a tool that could bring extraordinary value to my life and my business.

After several years of working 65-70 hours a week, with no vacations and very little social life, I found myself

When work is play, you are able to fully engage in the work itself.

wired, harried, and stressed-out. With some urging from a friend, I went kicking and screaming to a Workaholics Anonymous (WA) meeting. After only a few sessions, I came to realize that WA could help me get my life and my play back. I'm grateful for Workaholics Anonymous because it gave me the foundation for learning how to take control of my work, rather than my work controlling me. I also got a revelation that working all the time is not the same as being productive. (Along this theme, I recommend checking out Justin Ever's article "All Work and No Play Makes a Company Unproductive," in the August 5, 2007, issue of *U.S. News & World Report*.)

WHY PLAY AT WORK?

When work is play, you are able to fully engage in the work itself. It begins to not feel like work, but rather like play. When I play at work, I notice that my mind is freed up from too narrow a concentration and my thinking has room to take on a fresh and creative perspective.

A person with play in his life is not only able to get more work done, but is better able to see new insights, concepts, and even innovation in his work.

Playing at work also brings out our imagination.

Dr. Stuart Brown, trained in general and internal medicine, psychiatry, and clinical research, and founder of NIFP, has been studying and researching the science of play for several years. He and his council of advisors are on the cutting edge of researching the value and effects of playing at work. Their research on human play has begun to reveal its advantages to individuals, leaders, organizations, educators, and parents in creating transformational differences in the workplace, schools, and individuals' lives. NIFP envisions the science of human play becoming a recognized subject in the scientific community.

Playing at work also brings out our imagination. Albert Einstein asserted that "imagination is more important than knowledge." In fact, imagination energizes us to move toward innovation, gain insights into problems, and develop solutions. These are necessary benefits every organization needs from its workers in order to remain competitive. A recognized expert, advisor, and forecaster of trends for Fortune 500 companies, Faith Popcorn describes our economy as one that is also driven by innovation.

JUMP-START YOUR PLAYING POWER

What activities could you begin doing to turn on your playing power at work? Here are five to get you started.

#1 BREAK OUT

Ever hear the saying "curiosity killed the cat"? Well, it didn't and it won't kill you either. A lack of curiosity, however, *can* kill your creative spirit. Begin your workday with eyes of curiosity and wonder. You can do it even if you've been in the same job for 20 years. It's going to take breaking out to adjust your expectations. On Monday morning, when you are walking through the front door of your workplace, what are your expectations? Are you expecting it to be the same old ho hum, or are you excited about what may be?

Come on, we all did it when we were kids. I remember every evening during summer break, I would catch lightning bugs. I would put them in a clear glass jar with holes punched in the top. Then I'd observe them lighting up as if I had never seen them do this before. What once fascinated you about your work? How could you do the same tasks in a different way? When you work with fresh eyes, you will discover many things to be excited and even contented about. Curiosity opens the door for imagination and new ideas.

When you work with fresh eyes, you will discover many things to be excited and even contented about.

#2 **POWER PAUSE**

Do you remember how you used to laugh and giggle as a child? When playing with friends, children giggle 400 times a day, compared to 17 times a day for adults. Some of us learned from well-meaning adults to separate our laughter from everyday life. As a child, I heard, "Stop that giggling," and "Wipe that grin off of your face." Like so many other adults, as I grew up I began to not laugh as much at life. Instead I learned to laugh at "appropriate" times, like when I watched a movie, or saw a

Laughter helps to create joy on the inside of us. If we do it long enough, it will show on the outside too.

comedian at a comedy club, or when someone said something funny or told a joke. It just wasn't kosher to allow a spirit of laughter to permeate my life. If I did, I would not be viewed as being an adult, but rather as childish. It would do us all extreme good to pull back from these past erroneous conceptions. Go for it like you used to when you were five years old. At age five, I giggled all the time, especially if it wasn't funny. Laughter is the voice of joy. Laughter helps to create joy on the inside of us. If we do it long enough, it will show on the outside too.

In 2002, I had a revelation about my childhood laughter. Since then I laugh throughout my workday, not just when something funny happens. I laugh when I say or do something stupid. I laugh when others say or do something stupid. I laugh when the pressure is on and when it's not. I laugh when I hear or see something funny and when I don't. I laugh at my own jokes even when the joke is not funny. I make it a point to laugh at work every day. My laugh is so infectious that people began to come up to me and tell me they loved my laugh.

I even incorporated laughter in a speech for one of my non-profit clients. It was well received, yet I didn't think it would work with corporate clients. Then my mentor, Keith Harrell, commented, "Are you using laughter in your speaking? If you aren't, you're not being yourself." After Keith's comments, I took the risk. Now laughter has become a signature part of my presentations.

#3 STOP TO PLAY

When you're stressed, tired, overloaded, or pressured, take a "STOP to play" break. You're probably familiar with Dr. Roger Sperry's right-brain, left-brain behavioral trait theory for which he won the Nobel Prize in 1981. According to Sperry's research, the logical behavior traits are performed on the left side of the brain on the conscious level, while intuitive behavior functions on the right side of the brain at the subconscious level.

I do a similar play escape at work by going to the beach. When I'm experiencing the STOPs—stress,

Consider taking a STOP break two to three times a day.

tiredness, overload, and pressure—I stop working and "go" to the beach. I look at pictures of my favorite beach on St. John, Virgin Islands, and imagine myself walking on the sand. I feel my toes in the water, then my ankles, and then I'm waist-deep, until finally I am totally submerged in the warm water. After a couple of minutes of beach play, I am relaxed and better able to get re-submerged in whatever I was working on before I took this brief break.

Consider taking a STOP break two to three times a day. You will be amazed at how stopping for three to five minutes in this way will make you feel both relaxed and energized.

#4 PLAY OUT YOUR SOLUTIONS

Another way to incorporate play in the workplace is in your meetings. Michael Begeman, a meeting expert, was having a meeting with a group of executives. Each executive was given two toys—a meeting network mouse pad and a squeeze pad. Without being prompted, the executives played with these toys for the entire meeting. When one person would say something that another person didn't like, the second person would throw a ball across the table. Begeman believes the more you involve the whole person in a meeting, the more people will learn and the more of that learning they will retain.

When the weather is favorable, have your meetings outside in the open air instead of in the boardroom. If you have a corporate lawn, take blankets and refreshments with you. Start the meeting by looking up at the sky for a minute. Begin to wonder and imagine how things could be as you take on a different perspective of the issues at hand.

#5 PLAY BREAK

This final play activity is probably my favorite. The purpose of this activity is just to have fun. Coordinate having a play box in the break room or have your own personalized box in your office. The play box could be as simple as one of your desk drawers. Load it up with your favorite playthings. Have co-workers bring in their favorites too, such as Silly Putty, LEGOs, Nerf guns, pogo sticks, comic books, or anything else that could be played with on an individual basis. If you have fun playing with your toy, your mission was accomplished. Take a play break once a day.

Initially you may feel uncomfortable with the Player tool. You don't have to incorporate all the activities at once. Just do one activity for a month. Then pick another one and do it for a month. It won't be long before you have turned work into play.

EMPOWERMENT THOUGHTS

- I'm being my best self when I play at work.

- Instead of asking myself what to do about a problem, I ask, "How do I play out the solution to this problem?"

- If I find myself getting stressed, tired, overloaded, or pressured, I "STOP" to play.

- Plato said, "You can discover more about a person in an hour of play than in a year of conversation." I use the Player tool to play with others at work.

To receive your free in-depth
Empowerment Thought,
log on to www.ciemurray.com.

CHAPTER 6

Empowerment Tool of the Whyer
Discover Your Motivators

"We act as though comfort and luxury were the chief requirements of life, when all that we need to make us really happy is something to be enthusiastic about."
—CHARLES KINGSLEY

I'LL NEVER FORGET WHEN I FIRST heard the news report about an NFL player who turned in his football cleats and a $3.9 million contract for a rifle, an $18,000 annual salary, and an opportunity to be trained as a U.S. Army Ranger to fight in Afghanistan. The announcer said, "His name is Pat Tillman." I asked myself, "What would motivate Pat Tillman, or anybody else, to make such a trade to fight in a war?"

What would it take for you to be motivated and passionate about your work? A pay raise, a new office, recognition? If you got the pay raise, how long would your enthusiasm last? A week? A month? A year? What would it take to be enthusiastic about your work if you had to do it for a lifetime? For most people, it takes knowing what

The Empowerment Tool of the Whyer is your reason for wanting what you want.

their Whyer is. The Empowerment Tool of the Whyer is your reason for wanting what you want. Your Whyer is the engine, the motivating force that ignites your passion and enthusiasm for doing what you need to do to obtain the work life you want.

Rather than focusing on your goals and objectives, allow your Whyer to direct your efforts. Make your Whyer your impetus and inspiration to accomplish the goal. Allow your Whyer to become a motivating factor by keeping it in the forefront of your mind.

DOES YOUR WHYER PASS THE "BIG ENOUGH" TEST?

In Chapter Four, the Empowerment Tool of the Sayer, you were given an exercise to define a vision of your work life. Now that you have defined your vision, why do you want that vision? Is your Whyer big enough? Is it big enough to help sustain the energy and commitment necessary to accomplish your goal? Is your reason for wanting that vision to impress others, fulfill a childhood desire, or obtain material gain? If "yes," then it probably isn't big enough. Here are five criteria to test whether your Whyer is big enough. If it meets even one of these criteria, then it's big enough.

#1 DOES IT BENEFIT OTHERS?

Why do you want to achieve your goal? Is it to help someone other than yourself? There is nothing wrong with you getting rewarded, but when others benefit as well, it takes your enthusiasm up a notch. It helps you to maintain an energy level that empowers you every day. Do you want to close that sale just to meet your quota, or is it also to help customers make the best choice in purchasing a car? Does your motive help to spur your department or firm to be better, or is it to spur you toward achieving a promotion? Seek a motive that serves others or helps to make them better, and you're more likely to reach your goal.

Seek a motive that serves others or helps to make them better, and you're more likely to reach your goal.

In the 1993 movie *Rudy*, based on the true life story of Rudy Ruettiger, the main character dreams of playing football at Notre Dame. Although Rudy has no athletic ability, he relentlessly pursues this goal. When he goes to football practice, his everyday Whyer is simply to help his teammates perfect their offensive skills for the upcoming game. For two years, Rudy goes above and beyond his best self to help his teammates in preparing to be their best. Yet the coach never considers allowing Rudy to play in the game.

In his last year, Rudy approaches the coach about dressing and playing in one game. It is in this conversation that he reveals his big-enough Whyer for being willing to endure pain and injury during practice day after day. Rudy asks the coach to allow him to play because he wants to inspire his younger brothers, and his dad (who spent all of his working years in a coal mine), and everybody else who told him it couldn't be done. In the last game of the season, Rudy's teammates go to bat for him with the coach, and Rudy achieves his goal of playing football at Notre Dame.

#2 DOES IT STIR YOUR PASSION?

When you think about your Whyer, does it ignite fire, zeal, excitement, intensity? Do you think and talk about your vision all the time? Do you find it impossible to put it out of your mind?

What would motivate someone to launch a new business the next day after retiring from a 36-year career in the hospitality industry? Vicki Gordon retired on June 30, 2008, and on July 1st she launched Collins Gordon Group. Her big-enough Whyer was the opportunity to unite her two passions—corporate social responsibility and giving back to the community. Her mission, Gordon commented, is to "work with corporations and organizations to help them integrate and create a business strategy that delivers both business results and creates positive social change in the world."

#3 IS IT DONE OUT OF HONOR OR RESPECT FOR A CAUSE?

Pat Tillman, mentioned earlier, played the safety position for the Arizona Cardinals, breaking his team record with 224 tackles. A few months after the terroristic attacks were made on the United States on September 11, 2001, Pat Tillman enlisted as a U.S. Army Ranger. He wanted no fanfare, no publicity, over what he was doing. He just wanted to be treated like any other soldier. Why? Because he was motivated by a big-enough Whyer. A big-enough Whyer to honor his country, to fight for its

Does your motive help to spur your department or firm to be better or to help customers in some capacity?

ideals, privileges, and freedoms. Honor was big enough to move Pat to give up his privileged life-style as a professional football player. Big enough to give up his $3.9 million contract. Big enough to leave his new wife of just a few weeks. Big enough to give his life. Pat Tillman died on April 24, 2004, on a mountain road near Sperah, Afghanistan.

#4 IS IT PURPOSE DRIVEN?

Does your motive help to spur your department or firm to be better or to help customers in some capacity? Does your Whyer provide an opportunity to fulfill an important mission or purpose other than your own? Bessie Locke discovered her life's purpose when she was presented with an opportunity to help children.

In the early 1890s, Locke visited a kindergarten for impoverished children. Although an advocate for social justice from the heart, she was skeptical that this type of schooling would be of much help to these children. When she was invited back six months later, she was astonished at the progress the children had made. It was during this visit that Locke embraced kindergartens and became a primary advocate in the adopting of kindergartens as a discipline in the education of children in America.

She founded the National Kindergarten Association, using it as a platform to push for a national kindergarten bill in Congress. The bill was never adopted, but as a result of her efforts the Federal Bureau of Education created a Kindergarten division in 1912. She remained a kindergarten advocate up until her death in 1952. It is believed that due to her relentless efforts, kindergartens are an integral part of the education system in America today.

#5 ARE YOU FED UP?

Do you have an intense desire because you're fed up with the status quo? Are you moved to action because a situation is upsetting to you? Twenty-seven-year-old June Arunga was fed up with the state of poverty in her homeland of Africa. She set out to do something about it. Recently, Arunga launched Black Star Lines (BSL), a banking service

Without a big-enough Whyer, you are more likely to quit taking action toward achieving your goal before it manifests.

for strapped business owners in Africa. Utilizing the telecom infrastructure in Africa, BSL was able to make banking services both mobile and affordable. Within two months from BSL's launch, more than 500 vendors enrolled. BSL is making inroads to alleviating poverty in Africa by giving poor vendors access to a global market they once had no access to. Poor African vendors are now learning to put their talents to work, provide business solutions, and compete in the global economy.

BENEFITS OF THE BIG-ENOUGH WHYER

There are several benefits for taking the time to identify a big-enough Whyer. For one thing, it empowers you to concentrate on what's most important and let go of the small stuff. Your big-enough Whyer ignites enthusiasm, and enthusiasm enlarges your perception of your work situations. It will give your work new meaning—a meaning of satisfaction and love for what you're doing. You'll begin to approach your work with more energy, caring, and attitude. Your big-enough Whyer will enable you to lay aside any drudgery you have about your work and those you work with. Rather than enduring your work until you reach the goal, you can now enjoy it all the way through. You'll become more productive and valuable to yourself and to your organization.

Another benefit is that your big-enough Whyer can give you the internal fuel to keep going when the going gets tough. Unfortunately, most people go to work every day without a big-enough Whyer. They're just floating, drifting through life. Without a big-enough Whyer, you are more likely to quit taking action toward achieving your goal before it manifests. With a big-enough Whyer, you will be more able to stay working in the present moment, because you are inspired to do your work.

When you focus on a big-enough Whyer, you'll begin to view your work life as a means to provide meaningful service to others, whether it's clients, the public, customers, constituents, employees, or associates. Your Whyer can help turn dull, uninspiring, unchallenging work into stimulating, engaging work that makes your heart sing.

EMPOWERMENT THOUGHTS

- When I lists my goals at the start of the day, I also list my Whyers beside them.

- I shift my motives for working, from focusing on myself to being of service to someone else. When I do, I am more valuable to myself, my workplace, and the world.

- If I am unenthused about my work life, I'll re-examine my Whyer to make it big enough.

To receive your free in-depth
Empowerment Thought,
log on to www.ciemurray.com.

CHAPTER 7

Empowerment Tool of the Thanker
Loving and Liking It

"We must like what we have
when we don't have what we like."

—ROGER DE BUSSY-RABUTIN

I HAD A BUSINESS MEETING with a client in his suburban corporate offices in Alpharetta, Georgia. As I waited for him to retrieve me from the lobby, I noticed how jazzy their offices were decorated. When we were walking to the conference room, I noticed that the rest of the work facilities were coordinated with the lobby to give an airy, vibrant atmosphere to the workplace. I complimented the client on their great decor. He said, "Oh yeah, it is nice, but I hardly ever notice it anymore." I'm willing to bet that when this client first began working there, he noticed the decor a lot. But now it barely enters his thoughts.

How are you thinking about your work life? Are your thoughts similar to the ones you had when you first started working there? Remember when you got the phone call offering you the job, and how thankful you were? Along

The Empowerment Tool of the Thanker is being grateful for what you have, even when you don't have what you want.

with the gratitude came joy and thrill. You may have gone out to celebrate with friends and even bought them drinks because you were so thankful.

When's the last time you expressed gratitude for your workplace? Now, you might be saying, "Why should I be grateful? I don't like working here anymore." Because even when you're in the midst of a work environment you don't like, your thankfulness empowers you with joy. What is joy? It is an attitude of gladness and gratefulness that is not dependent on whether circumstances are good or bad. Joy is a choice. When you use your Thanker tool to turn on the power of joy, *you* become empowered.

The Empowerment Tool of the Thanker is being grateful for what you have, even when you don't have what you want. You may not have the work life you want, but you do have a job. Or maybe you don't have a job right now, but you are receiving an unemployment check. Or perhaps your unemployment benefits have stopped, but you are physically healthy. You get the point.

Thankfulness kick-starts your enthusiasm and changes your mood. It means taking the step to say you're thankful, even if you don't feel grateful. It helps you rethink your Thinker (thoughts in the head and heart) to be thankful until the feeling shows up.

In the early years of my career I had a job I loved, but my micro-managing boss was driving me nuts. Because of that, I just couldn't seem to feel grateful. One day on my lunch hour, I drove over to the state unemployment office. I walked in and saw at least a hundred people standing in line who did not have a job. Well, I got grateful real fast. Perhaps you too have a job you like, but don't like the people you work with. Start saying, "I'm grateful for my job." Then add to your statement, "I'm thankful for my job and a $10,000 pay raise." The Thanker tool is not just about being thankful for what you have, but for all you are going to have. When you say thank you for the $10,000 pay increase, you have set your will to receive it.

The Thanker tool is not just about being thankful for what you have, but for all you are going to have.

TOP TEN OCCASIONS FOR USING THE THANKER TOOL

#10 WHEN MORALE IS LOW.

I have coached managers who felt that saying "thank you" to their subordinates was not necessary. Their primary rationale was that workers are getting paid to do a job and that they should do a great job every day because that's what they are paid to do. But remember, we're dealing with human beings who have emotions. Most people get a boost from hearing "thank you," which results in greater productivity. Cal Darden, a senior vice president at UPS, knows this firsthand. He personally calls star employees when he receives reports of their stellar performance. "After you do that, they'll run through a wall for you," said Darden.[*]

#9 WHEN YOU'VE BECOME FAT.

Thankfulness enables you to better handle being FAT—**f**rustrated, **a**ngry, or **t**ired—at work.

#8 WHEN YOU ARE IN A STATE OF DISCONTENTMENT WITH YOUR JOB.

Many times discontentment occurs when we begin to compare ourselves with others. Barbara, your associate, got a challenging project. Now you have become dissatisfied with what you have. The

---

[*] Morey Stettner, "The Honest Heart Brand of Leadership," *Investors Business Daily* (May 17, 2004).

Thanker tool helps to eliminate the discontentment that arrives as a result of ongoing comparisons.

#7 WHEN YOU ARE WORRYING ABOUT THE FUTURE.

Thankfulness helps you to stay in the present moment, taking one day at a time. Do you have a big project with multiple tasks to perform in a short period of time? Begin giving thanks for what you were able to accomplish today. Do the same thing the next day, and the next, until you complete the project. You will be amazed at how you will be able to accomplish more each day because your worrying about the future will begin to subside. There is power working in the here and now.

#6 THANKFULNESS CAN TURN A LEMON OF A JOB SITUATION INTO LEMONADE.

Phyllis was excited about starting her new job. Soon after her start date, she learned that her office was one of the worst-producing offices for her entire organization. Most of her new co-workers complained about how they would be more motivated if only management would give them more recognition and appreciation.

When October rolled around, the office was still in last place. There were rumors that many of

Start giving value to who you are and what you have by giving yourself a pat on the back...

the staff positions were going to be outsourced. That's when Phyllis asked management if she could coordinate a Thanksgiving program celebration in the office. At the event, she had several colleagues share what they were grateful for. One person told how she had been homeless and was so grateful that she had a job and thus the means to raise her family. Another associate expressed her gratitude toward Phyllis for coordinating the program. She said, "The program allowed me to view my co-workers as family. We let our hair down, cooked, baked, sang songs, laughed together, and hugged like family." The program helped workers realize that the office had many attributes to be grateful for. Gradually the atmosphere began to shift from complacency to assertiveness. Three years later, Phyllis's office is now among the company's top-producing in the country.

Instead of their work being outsourced, everybody got to keep their jobs.

#5 WHEN YOU ARE FEELING UNDERVALUED AND UNAPPRECIATED.

You enlarge yourself and your value when you give thanks to yourself. Start giving value to who you are and what you have by giving yourself a pat on the back, even when no one else notices the great work you are doing.

#4 WHEN YOU ARE EXPERIENCING SAP—STRESS, ANXIETY, AND PRESSURE.

When an associate of mine would become stressed and the pressure built up on her job, she would quit. Eventually she learned that instead of allowing the pressure around her to move her to quit, she could alleviate the uncomfortable feelings by giving thanks. She said, "Thanksgiving helps me to release the stress." She went from changing jobs ten times in the medical field to having only one job for all of last year.

#3 WHEN YOU NEED TO GET FOCUSED ON THE BIG PICTURE.

So many times we get embroiled in the small stuff, like getting frustrated waiting for a sign-off on a project or doing a requisition to get paper clips. We begin to

When I realized that my competitive jealousy was hindering me from doing my best, I shifted the focus to my own performance by giving thanks for what I already had.

neglect to see what's right about our work environment. Focusing on the big stuff helps you accept that things don't have to run smoothly for you to enjoy your work life. If you look at the big picture, you'll surely find a lot more right than wrong.

#2 WHEN COMPETITIVE OFFICE JEALOUSY CREEPS IN.

When I first started in radio sales, I used to envy the top sales producers. I found it difficult to stay focused on my own work efforts, because I was constantly looking over at them. When I realized that my competitive jealousy was hindering me from doing my best, I shifted the focus to my own performance by giving thanks for what I already had. Every time I closed a sale, no matter the size, I gave thanks. I even started celebrating with co-workers on their new sales. Eventually, I too became a top producer.

#1 ANYTIME.

Thanksgiving ignites the subconscious to move quicker in bringing your desires into existence. As the psalmist says, "It is a good thing to give thanks."

SAY YOUR ABCs

How do you exercise your Thanker tool? Some people use journals to write down the things they are grateful for. My favorite is to say my ABCs. When one of the aforementioned workplace occasions occurs, I say my ABCs to activate my joy. To help stir up your thoughts, I've listed my ABC workplace Thankers. I especially use them when I'm feeling FAT—frustrated, angry, or tired—or when I'm experiencing SAP—stress, anxiety, or pressure. I simply go through the ABCs, saying something I can be thankful for, for each letter of the English alphabet, starting with "A."

A = Alive. I'm alive this very moment.

B = Balance. I'm becoming more and more balanced in my thinking. My actions are catching up. Every day last week I stopped work at 6:00 p.m.

C = Clients and Customers. Thank God for clients. They pay the company's bills and enable me to get a paycheck.

D = Development and Growth. Many of my consulting clients are developing and growing from the principles I teach.

E = Energy to get the job done.

F = Fax machine that works.

G = God, who is always there for me.

H = Hug from my husband today.

I = Imagination to visualize the possibilities.

J = Job I love most of the time.

K = Kindness from my neighbor's cat.

L = Laughter allows me to let go of my mistakes and hang-ups.

M = Meetings and conferences that allow me to meet and share encouragement with many people at one time.

N = Networking events. These provide opportunities to meet new people and stay connected to existing relationships.

O = **Opportunity** to help those in need.

P = **People** to work with who help challenge me to grow.

Q = **Quality** of life and living that I experience in the USA.

R = **Relationships** new and old, without which my life would be empty.

S = **Speaking,** which allows me to put voice and sound to who I am, to express my needs, to communicate with others, and to share encouragement with them.

T = **Tasks** that provide a sense of accomplishment as well as those that are mundane but just need to be done.

U = **Unfolding** of my journey one day at a time.

V = **Vendors** who do good work at reasonable prices.

W = **World Wide Web,** which allows me to do business in an inexpensive and expansive manner.

X = **X-ing** out the past, which allows me to focus on the good that is to come.

Y = Years spent living and loving my life.

Z = Zest for life is partly due to doing work that benefits others.

Usually by the time I reach "M," I'm no longer feeling FAT or experiencing SAP. If I'm not back in a space of joy by this time, I just keep saying my ABCs, starting over again with new thanks. Now fill in the blanks below for your ABC workplace Thankers.

A= _____

B= _____

C= _____

D= _____

E= _____

F= _____

G= _____

H= _____

I= _____

J= _____

K= _____

L= _____

M= _____

N= _____

O= _____

P= _____

Q= _____

R= _____

S= _____

T= _____

U= _____

V= _____

W= _____

X= _____

Y= _____

Z= _____

Your Thanker tool is being grateful for what you have when you don't have what you want. Start giving thanks for what you have and even for what you don't have yet but would like to have. When you do, you stimulate your subconscious into motion to turning your "don't haves" into "haves" a reality. As the epistle says, "Give thanks in all things." What are you waiting for? Start giving thanks now.

EMPOWERMENT THOUGHTS

- I give thanks for what is good and right at work, rather than complaining about those things that are not.

- When my boss, employees, or co-workers do something kind, rewarding, or beneficial, I make the effort to tell them "thank you."

- When I begin to feel discontented with my workplace, I say my ABCs.

- I give thanks for those things I don't yet have. When I do this, I stimulate my subconscious into motion to turning my "don't haves" into "haves."

*To receive your free in-depth
Empowerment Thought,
log on to www.ciemurray.com.*

For more information,
email us at
info@ciemurray.com
or visit us on the web at
www.ciemurray.com